Keep Blessing Us, *Ultima*

A Teaching Guide for

Bless Me, Ultima by

Rudolfo Anaya

Abelardo Baeza, Ph.D.

EAKIN PRESS ★ AUSTIN, TEXAS

FIRST EDITION

Copyright © 1997
By Dr. Abelardo Baeza

Published in the United States of America
By Eakin Press
A Division of Sunbelt Media, Inc.
P.O. Box 90159
Austin, Tx 78709

2 3 4 5 6 7 8 9

ISBN 1-57168-158-2

This book is dedicated
in memory of
my beloved sister,
Lily Tarango.

I am grateful to the following people who helped me with my book:

Eileen Swiers and Rhonda Austin, secretaries in the Sul Ross State University Department of Languages and Literature;

Paul Olsen in the SRSU print shop, for his help;

Dr. Felipe Ortega y Gasca and Dr. Nelson C. Sager, for their advice and moral support;

Dr. David Cockrum, Vice-President for Academic Affairs at SRSU, for his encouragement and words of wisdom;

Professor Rudolfo Anaya, for giving me the chance of a lifetime to work with him.

Rudolfo Anaya

Table of Contents

Rudolfo Anaya

Preface

The idea of writing my own textbook had crossed my mind many times, but the proverbial lack of time kept me from sitting down and penning some thoughts. When Custom Publishers mailed an attractive packet with interesting ideas for designing a text, I made the time to do it.

My faithful filing cabinets hold many folders with materials from my Children's and Adolescent Literature course, a class designed for prospective public school teachers and children's psychologists. I went through each folder, pulling out handouts and bibliographies that are interesting and informative to my students.

In no time at all, I had enough suggestions to send to Associate Editor Marianne Dombroski, who has been most helpful with this project. I explained to her that I wanted a text that would have materials for all levels — from kindergarten through high school. How many times had I received requests from both teachers and student teachers for a particular poem or short story that the basal readers in the public schools often fail to include?

With this thought in mind, I began to arrange the original table of contents, which brought a reaction from Marianne. "Too long!" was her comment, indicating that my book would be about 800 pages long. I went back to the drawing board, or in this case, computer table, and re-designed the offerings. This time I thought of the students, rather than the teachers. My whole attitude and approach changed once I surveyed my own students and heard their demands and requests.

The result is a potpourri of classical and contemporary selections for children and adolescents. Because of the interest in multiculturalism today, I included a wide variety of authors and genres. Literature is a reflection of society, and anthologies such as this one must create a beautiful mirror for young minds. I am certain that my book will do just that.

However, I cannot take all the credit. There have been many people who have helped me with my popular Children's and Adolescent Literature, mainly the students with majors in Interdisciplinary Studies and English. They survey the anthologies and read an abundance of children's poetry, short stories, fables, historical fiction, science fiction, drama, rhymes, nonsense verses, and folktales. The adolescent literature blocks include poetry, drama, short fiction, novel, and essay.

Furthermore, I call on a number of people who are experts in respective fields important to the study of children's and adolescent literature. My sincere thanks goes to people such as Bob Hext, SRSU professor of art, who presents an interesting workshop on the writing and illustration of children's books; Eleanor Wilson, director of Library Services, whose lectures on the controversial issue of censorship raise awareness among my students; Jo Reesing, a seasoned second grade teacher at Alpine Elementary School, who perennially brings her delightful students to visit my university classroom while studying Wilson Rawls' classics, *Where the Red Fern Grows* and *The Summer of the Monkeys*; and all the professional men and women who have served as judges for my annual Creative Writing Contest, analyzing the beautiful and original books that my students write and illustrate.

As I look back over a career that spans twenty-five years, I can say that I am proud of the work that I have done in my two areas of study — English and Spanish. I have discovered that a person who has a good literary background in the primary grades will more than likely have a positive attitude toward reading and writing as adolescents and adults.

This theory is evidenced by the first assignment which I give in my class — to write a short composition on the first book which my students read as children. Lamentably, many do not remember. Could it be that their backgrounds are weak and incomplete? Many of my students can give me a description of the plot, but not the author's name. Others apologize and tell me heart-wrenching stories about their writing experiences in the primary levels.

The result is obvious — a negative attitude toward literature and its purpose. Studying the works of classic writers such as Hans Christian Andersen, Gertrude Chandler Warner, Theodor Geisel (better known to readers as Dr. Seuss), Judy Blume, and the famous Grimm Brothers means little to those pupils who have read little or nothing. A wealth of enjoyment and awareness of children and their worlds has been lost.

However, I tell my students that they can retrieve those precious moments in my class through reading and study. The children's literature market has provided us with beautiful editions of classics by Perrault, Robert Browning, Lewis Carroll, Beatrix Potter, and others. Contemporary writers such as Maurice Sendak, Eric Carle, Charlotte Zolotow, Betsy Byars, and Susan Lowell, and Rudolfo Anaya are creating new books each year, examining timely, interesting, sometimes controversial themes such as social ostracism, physical transformations, and violence.

— Abelardo Baeza, Ph.D

Rudolfo Anaya: Man of Aztlán

Meeting Ultima: An Introduction

Being asked by Rudolfo Anaya to write a teaching guide for *Bless Me, Ultima* is an honor I will cherish the rest of my life.

I have admired this gentleman and his writing talent for many years now, having read the novel in a Chicano Literature course at Texas Tech University. Dr. Edmundo Garcia-Giron assigned *Ultima* to me as my semester project, with instructions to find as much information on the book and its author as possible. Does one question his professor's motives while enrolled in a Ph.D. program?

With this thought in mind, I began an extensive search in the Tech library, collecting information from books and periodicals. One book that stands out in my mind is *Chicano Authors* by Juan Bruce-Novoa; I discovered an interesting biographical sketch on Anaya, followed by an interview that was most useful in discussing his views about writing and its relationship to the human spirit.

The project was well received by the class during my oral presentation. While my fellow classmates wrote papers on Tomas Rivera, Estela Portillo, and Alurista that offered good information on the Chicano movement, my paper opened a new vision into the metaphysical world of Rudy Anaya. His novel is one of few to use the stream-of-consciousness approach as seen through the dreams of the little hero, Tony Marez, who perceives his birth into the world in Guadalupe, a small farming community in New Mexico. Anaya presents Tony's perceptions of the good and evil forces that exist in the world, as well as his questions about death and life after death. His intelligence and insights amaze all those around him, including his teacher, Miss Maestas, and Ultima, his mentor, making him look like a young Jesus in the temple, addressing the sages of old.

Furthermore, I pointed out the complexities of the story as it spins into numerous sub-plots and introduces such unforgettable characters as the devil incarnate, Tenorio Trementina, and his evil daughters; Rosie, the town's painted lady, very reminiscent of Belle Watling in Margaret Mitchell's *Gone With the Wind*, and "La Pintada" in Mariano Azuela's *Los de Abajo* (*The Underdogs*); Tío Lucas, the ill-fated *campesino* who seeks help from the wise old *curandera*; Father Byrnes, the charismatic Catholic priest who uses interesting paradoxes to teach the children the concepts of life, death, and eternity; Narciso, the town drunk who defends Ultima to the end; Florence, the little *güerito* with an existential philosophy of life that reminds any American literature aficionado of Hemingway's Nick Adams in the famous short story "Three Day Blow"; and the infamous gang — Horse, Bones, the Vitamin Kid, Cico, Samuel, and Abel — the "little men" who bring to mind those young heroes of S.E. Hinton's *The Outsiders*, all in pursuit of survival, friendships, and adventure.

With projects such as this one, I learned the true meaning of literary criticism and scholarship. I yearned for more insights into the world of multicultural literature. I promised myself that one day, I, too, would teach such a course. After completing my degree, I returned to my position on the English faculty at Sul Ross State University. To my surprise, I discovered that the chairmanship had changed hands. I approached the new *jefe*, Dr. Robert Bass, with the idea of teaching a Chicano Literature class. The curriculum had to change, I insisted, and had to include at least one multicultural class. He agreed. With my file from Dr. Garcia-Giron's class, I set out to gather materials for the course. *Bless Me, Ultima* was my first choice for the novel. I nestled it among the poetry, *cuentos*, and dramas written by Abelardo Delgado, Jose Angel Gutierrez, Joseph Flores, Tomas Rivera, Luis Valdez, and Estela Portillo, who gave a fantastic dramatic reading in my Chicano

Literature course last summer of her critically acclaimed play, "The Day of the Swallows."

Perusing my files, I found the original class roll for that course. Thirty-eight students enrolled in it and helped me to develop it into one of the most popular courses in the Department of Languages and Literature. My students have all gone on to teach the *cuentos*, dramas, poetry, essays, and novels that were presented to them in Chicano Literature. I hear from them at various times during the school year; I receive cards or letters which express their thoughts and frustrations. I write back — and remind them about the *ganas*, or desire, that they developed in my class. They are encouraged never to give up, even if others criticize them and keep them from using their materials because of social and academic guidelines and pressures. They ask for help and resources to enrich their classes, and I always comply.

The purpose of this study is to share with others my experiences with Rudy Anaya and his novel. At Sul Ross State University, I can reach my students through my classes and seminars. However, I want to seek out those who are not able to come to the university — those dedicated, hard-working educators who are in the public schools, attempting to create ideas, values, and independent thinking within their students. If they have not considered including *Bless Me, Ultima* as part of their curricula, for whatever reasons, they should be encouraged to do so because this novel, in my opinion, is the *catalyst* of Chicano Literature. It is destined to become a classic and join the ranks of those novels written by Hemingway, Steinbeck, and Fitzgerald during the earlier part of the twentieth century.

Through the novel and the teaching guide, I hope that both teachers and students will have their lives enriched as mine has been. Most of all, I want them to feel that they have indeed been blessed by one of the most noble and enduring women ever created in American literature.

— Abelardo Baeza, Ph.D.
Sul Ross State University / Alpine, Texas
1997

xiii

Ladies and Gentlemen, Meet Rudy Anaya

Principally because of his first novel, *Bless Me, Ultima* (1972), Rudolfo Anaya is considered a major contemporary Mexican-American writer. The book, one of the few Chicano literary best-sellers, appears on high school and college curricula, holds an important place in the landscape of Chicano literary criticism, and (with some of his other novels) has been translated into German and Polish. The book's merit and market success have allowed Anaya to enjoy popularity simultaneously with relative critical acclaim. Since 1972 he has published numerous novels and coedited several anthologies.

Anaya was born to Martin and Rafaelita Mares Anaya on 30 October 1937, in Pastura, a village lying south of Santa Rosa in eastern New Mexico. He attended public schools in Santa Rose and Albuquerque despite an extended hospitalization for a spinal injury he suffered as a youth. He earned a B.A. (1963) and M.A. (1968) in English from the University of New Mexico, and he also has an M.A. (1972) in guidance and counseling from the same institution. In 1966 he married Patricia Lawless, who is also trained in guidance and counseling.

From 1963 to 1970 Anaya taught in the Albuquerque public schools. He left to become director of counseling at the University of Albuquerque. His appointment in the Department of English at the University of New Mexico began in 1974. He has received numerous awards and fellowships, including an honorary doctorate from the University of Albuquerque, the New Mexico Governor's Award for Excellence, and the President's National Salute to American Poets and Writers in 1980. Perhaps the most important of his honors is the Premio Quinto Sol awarded to *Bless Me, Ultima*, for it was his first national literary honor and a harbinger of later recognition, including grants from the National Endowment for the Arts and the national Chicano Council of Higher Education, and a Kellogg Fellowship.

To read Anaya's work is to encounter a preoccupation with, as he describes it, "instinct and the dark blood in which it dwells"(*MELUS*, Spring 1984). The bringing of instinct to light is both an artistic and a moral imperative for Anaya, who perceives the writer's role in shamanistic terms. He points this out with painstaking care in his gloss to his *The Silence of the Llano: Short Stories* (The Silence of the Plain: Short Stories, 1982):

> The storyteller tells stories for the community as well as for himself. The story goes to the people to heal and reestablish balance and harmony, but the process of the story is also working the same magic on the storyteller . . . [who] must be free and honest, and . . . must remain independent of the whims of groups. Remember, the shaman, the *curandero* [folk healer], the mediator do their work for the people, but they live alone.

Anaya is also concerned with integrating into his work the Jungian ideas associated with intuition and feeling. Nowhere in his work is the integration of subjective insight as effective or inspired as in his first novel.

A Word from Rudolfo Anaya

I am very glad to learn that you have completed your study guide for the teaching of *Bless Me, Ultima*. I know you have been teaching the novel since it first appeared on the scene. You are probably one of a handful of scholars and teachers who has given the novel such loving care and critical attention.

Your students, and the teachers of Texas, will profit immensely from the study guide. The more critical comments and letters from teachers and students I receive, the more I humbly agree that the novel is more complex than appears on the surface. It helps to have a guide who has chartered the waters, who knows the culture, the symbols, the dreams, and the characters of the novel. You are such a guide. And your study guide is the raft on which students of the novel can climb aboard to better understand the work.

So, like a rafting trip down the Río Grande, I invite everyone who reads you guide to settle in for a revealing trip. They're in good hands with you at the helm, guiding them through the intricacies of the novel.

You have done education in Texas a great service with your quarter century of teaching, and you have done contemporary Chicano and Chicana literature the same service by believing in our work. You knew the voice should be heard, so you took the stories, poems, songs, cuentos and novels in to the classroom and created a new curriculum. All of us thank you for that. because of you, and teachers like you, Mexican Americans know their literature, history and culture better. And you have helped those who are not Chicanos look into our literature and become not only aficionados of the literature, but better neighbors.

La frontera, that space you know so well, is a fascinating region. You have taught its children, and so you have enriched the people. Your work has borne fruit. I get calls and letters from all over Texas from your former students. All learned to read literature critically and with amor in your classes.

This study guide is only one step in your career. Yes, I'm very proud of it. It will be your voice in those classess where you personally cannot mentor the students. It will guide future students of literature, presenting ideas for them to wrestle with, and then challenging them to think for themselves, to come to their own conclusions. That's what a good guide does, nuture the students and then free them so they take wing. Or to continue my metaphor, so they can one day guide the raft down the Río Grande.

Comtemporary Chicano/a literature is still young in this country. We have a rich oral tradition, and much history in newspaper publishing, but the books that a students can actually carry, read, learn to love are new. The study guides will help many understand our literature, history and culture. Thus we create a better world. Gracias for that new world you help create.

Tu amigo, Rudolfo Anaya

Teaching
Bless Me, Ultima

BLE𝒮𝒮 ME, ULTIMA

Rudolfo A. Anaya

A PUBLICATION OF TONATIUH INTERNATIONAL

DID YOU READ IT?

Teaching a novel is a challenge for any educator — at any level. Most of us have had the experience of selecting a book which is considered a must for junior or senior high school students, only to be confronted by groans and moans that arise when they see the number of pages! To us, as pedagogues of the written or spoken word, reading a good novel is an experience that lasts forever, but to students, the book is a 500-pound ball and chain in eye-straining print!

However, as a professor who has taught numerous novels in both English and Spanish courses through the years to both experienced and inexperienced readers, I recommend *Bless Me, Ultima* as a book which students will enjoy from the opening lines to the heart-wrenching ending. To provide students with a positive, unforgettable reading adventure, I encourage teachers to follow my personal steps in setting up the novel block.

THE PRE-NOVEL STAGE

1. **Set the stage for Rudy Anaya's novel by placing materials on your bulletin board.** I recommend clippings from newspapers or magazines (see Bibliography). If you want to be subliminal, you may try using pictures or drawings of juniper, pine, or cottonwood trees; owls, or *lechuzas* as they are called in Spanish; postcards with depictions of mountains, lakes, and horses, preferably in the Southwest. Students are visually oriented, as evidenced by their preoccupation with baseball cards, videos, MTV, and computerized games. Visual elements stir their curiosity.

1

2. **Prepare handouts on Rudy Anaya's life and works.** I simply started by collecting materials I found printed in newspapers, magazines, book jackets, pamphlets, and programs in manila folders, color-coding them according to content (i.e., *red* for biography, *green* for bibliography, and *white* for book reviews), and placing them in a cabinet labeled "Multi-cultural Literature." I suggest one handout per day to avoid waste and confusion. Tell students that they must keep all materials in order for their unit portfolio.

3. **Ask your students to bring 4x6 notecards to class.** They will prepare a notecard on each of the twenty-two chapters as they read and discuss the novel in class. All notecards will be placed in the portfolio at the end of the unit. The notecards will have the number of the chapter on the top line. Sample annotations can be found in this book under "Chapter Notes." They can also include names of characters, vocabulary, literary terms used (symbolism, irony, style, foreshadowing), and important pages. In essence, the students are creating their own study guides.

4. **If you have a video recording of Rudy Anaya's visit to Sul Ross State University and his mesmerizing talk before a large crowd, let your students watch part of the program.** This will allow them to meet him, hear his voice, and realize that the man on the screen is alive and well in Albuquerque, New Mexico. Most students have never met the authors of the books they read. They react when they have an opportunity to hear them and collect their autographs. In a telephone conversation which I had with Rudy Anaya on May 17, 1995, the author related that he had met a delegation from Fort Stockton, Texas, that had traveled to New Mexico for a conference. Rudy presented a reading from his newest novel. The visitors were delight-

ed to hear the presentation — and to meet him. "They realized at that time that I *am* real and *alive*," laughed Rudy.

I agree wholeheartedly. Teachers interpret the literature found in basal readers and anthologies, but nothing can be more effective than meeting and hearing the writers of the creative works which we as English teachers include in our syllabi.

5. **Present a short chronology of Anaya's life, but be careful not to drown them with trivia.** An English teacher who stresses small, insignificant data instead of important information about the author is asking for trouble. Students will lose interest if they spend too much time reading background notes instead of the novel itself. The Appendix has some of my favorite materials on Rudy Anaya.

6. **Give your students a bibliography of Anaya's works.** Allow students to see his collections of short stories, novels, children's stories, and drama. I recommend an exhibit of these books. My students become aware of Rudy's prolific writing experience when they see his books on a special table to the right side of my desk — or on the chalkboard rail behind me. Allow a few minutes before starting your class for students to browse through the books. This "free reading" concept need not be abandoned after elementary school. Make arrangements with your school librarian for setting up a special display of Rudy's works in the library. This type of reinforcement is most important for those students (and faculty members) who are reading his literature for the first time.

7. **Prepare a vocabulary list from each chapter. I recommend at least twenty to twenty-five words.** Have them pronounce the words aloud and then look up the definitions in their pocket dictionaries. This is a good activi-

ty for your students to do in pairs or groups of three. The lists will be included in their unit portfolios. They will use them in writing their essays at the end of the novel block.

"Behold the golden carp, Lord of the waters —"
(Bless Me Ultima, p. 105)

Reading *Bless Me, Ultima*

1. **Divide the novel into blocks (3–5 chapters in each block).** It is better to use this approach rather than to assign the entire book to be read during one weekend. With honors English classes and Gifted and Talented Programs, you may want to have 5-8 chapters in each block. Never force a student to read a novel. You must provide inspiration and motivation.

2. **Assign the students to read the chapters as listed.** You can design a short reading comprehension quiz to help them understand the story effectively (see samples listed in next section). Instead of administering the quiz at the beginning of the period, you may want to give it during the last phase of the lesson. Students detest the "pop" quiz concept, but they are more open to the evaluation approach. Their grades, as well as their levels of self-esteem, are stronger and more positive. Mine are told that in order

to make perfect scores, they must listen carefully during the discussions. Any student who has a perfect average on the quizzes will receive a special prize at the conclusion of the unit. These prizes can range from pocket dictionaries to pizzas! My students really like my choice of incentives. I have also exempted students from taking the final examination if they have perfect attendance and an average of 90 or better.

3. **Allow students to read specific passages aloud.** They need to hear another person's voice besides the teacher's. My students confess that they have not read aloud since their junior high school years. They are encouraged to read, especially the scenes which will be the most memorable. My favorite scene is Tony's first day in school. Rudy Anaya has written many good vignettes in his literature, but this one takes me back to my own first day of school. This reminiscing creates stimulating class discussions about first days in schools, impressionable teachers, and cultural traditions, such as Tony's lunch of "tacos de frijoles and a small jar of chile" in contrast to the sandwiches of white bread that he sees being eaten by his classmates.

4. **After each block is completed, divide the class into groups (3-4 in each group).** I call these "brainstorming sessions" and find them helpful in creating interest, promoting rapport among students, exchanging points of view, and providing interesting interpretations. Your experienced readers will offer good ideas and insights for those with limited reading backgrounds. Also, you may want to consider allowing them to answer the chapter questions during these sessions, with the understanding that the answers will be written and included in the portfolio. The questions become the study guide for the unit exam.

5. **If you are going to spend three to four weeks on**

the novel block, you can have the students submit their chapter notecards to you on Friday. These can be returned to them on Monday for inclusion in the portfolio. I encourage my students to become creative with their notecards; they can write, print, or type their cards. Artistic students can draw designs on the margins or on the back. These sketches can be symbolic of the contents read (examples: an owl, a medicinal herb, three clay dolls, a black horse, a rosary, a scapulary, or a Nativity scene).

6. **Have each student select a cultural code ("Zorro," "Cortez," "La Llorona,") and prepare a computerized progress chart for your bulletin board.** The chart will record the students' grades on quizzes, notecards, unit grade, and portfolio grade. I have done this for all my classes — and circumvent many questions and doubts, which can be a teacher's nightmare! As they complete an assignment, I post the grade or check mark; they can see their own progress. The codes are recorded in the gradebook, next to the students' names to ensure total anonymity. Their interest soars to the top! I have also found that posting grades in this manner creates good, clean competition, a real plus for any class. In no time at all, I see my students sitting outside in the sun — with their copies of *Ultima* next to their cans of Classic Coke and Snickers bars! I am a strong believer of the freedom of expression approach; I encourage questions and discussion. Nothing is more lethal to teachers than a class that is "DOA" — Dead on Arrival!

7. **Allow time for questions at all times during the reading of *Ultima*.** If the students have a difficult time understanding the significance of Tony's dreams (italicized in print for emphasis), explain the concept through the life-saving *Handbook to Literature* by C. Hugh Holman (7th Edition). His definitions, examples, and literary references

have saved many student grades. Above all, allow them to present their own views and interpretations. As teachers, we consider ourselves the ultimate authorities, at times losing sight of the reasons we are in the classrooms — to impart our knowledge to them in an open, impartial manner and to encourage independent thinking. At the university level, I encounter many students who are afraid to speak out in classes. They expect for me to lead the discussions and interpret the plot of the novel for them. They lack experience in critical reading and writing. A novel such as *Ultima* is perfect for developing these skills. It is interesting and challenging — a good vehicle for instilling proper reading habits among young readers!

8. **Avoid rushing the students through the novel block.** Time is secondary to understanding. Allow yourself a few extra days for reviews and discussions. *Ultima* is a penetrating novel, and will raise many questions from the students. When they realize that the story is told from the eyes of a child, your students will begin to appreciate the plot and parallel their questions to Tony's queries to those around him. They identify with Tony's friends and their lives. They laugh at Horse's escapades and react when they listen to Florence's account of his sad life and his pessimism.

9. **Write the names of the characters on the chalkboard from the first day of the unit.** Keep adding their names as they appear in the plot. These board notes will be part of their portfolio. Teaching students to take proper notes will be a valuable aid for them when they enroll in college or university level courses. One idea is to take a notecard, write the name of the character in question, and write a brief description of the person (clothes, mannerisms, habits, physical traits).

10. **Employ the talents of your bilingual students to**

translate the Spanish terms and expressions found in *Ul-tima.* You will be stressing the importance of bilingual-ism/biculturalism. You can insert a "mini" unit on Anaya's use of *calo,* or Spanglish — a regional dialect that combines colloquial Spanish and English — hence, the term "Tex-Mex," which I abhor! Consider consulting a text entitled *Colloquial Spanish: A Complete Language Course* by Untza Otaola Alday (first published in 1995 by Routledge) for de-finitions and examples of this hybrid form of Spanish. Stu-dents can create their own "mini" bilingual dictionaries as group projects. Again, you are encouraging group work and harmony among your students. You can display their dictionaries in your classroom or in the school library. In addition to their portfolios, you are giving them a valuable educational tool which they can carry with them into their other English classes. At the university level, I encourage my students to save their materials for their student teach-ing experience, which can be difficult for those who have never collected any literature or resources. Having your students write their own portfolios, dictionaries, creative projects (children's books, poetry books, or short story col-lections) will enable them to see their work in print. Most of all, they will see a justification for their work.

11. **Display the portfolios in your room or in the school library.** Allow your students to be creative. They can decorate their books with cultural symbols. Select a panel of judges to evaluate the books. Set up an Awards Ceremony to recognize the top five portfolios. I have giv-en cash prizes donated by the local bank or telephone company. These recognitions ignite the students' desire to improve their reading and writing skills.

12. **Assign the unit essay, using some of the ideas found in the Appendix.** Give your students at least *three* calendar days to write their compositions. They may use

their notes from the unit materials given to them. Encourage them to use the composition lab. You should specify that they must prepare a cover page and a two-level outline to accompany their papers (300-350 words).

13. **The unit exam can be part objective and part subjective (see sample in Appendix).** I interject quotes, puns, and "plays-on-words" drawn from the novel. Get creative! I insert humorous terms or expressions in the objective part. Rudy's novel has tremendously funny scenes — use them!

I suggest a *pilon*, or bonus, to help students make better grades. In the Hispanic culture, *el pilon*, equivalent of the famous baker's dozen in English, is commonplace. I follow the tradition. As a result, my students expect the bonus. It serves as a good incentive and an excellent ego booster.

Chapters 1–8

NOTES

CHAPTER 1

Ultima comes to live with the Marez family. The Old Woman is addressed as "La Grande." Tony's brothers are at war in Europe. Ultima brings her owl with her. We discover that she delivered all of the Marez children. Tony is mesmerized by her aura.

CHAPTER 2

Lupito kills the sheriff. Chavez seeks help from Gabriel Marez. Backed by a posse, Narciso attempts to bring Lupito to justice. The doomed war veteran is killed by the posse. Tony witnesses the massacre. Tony has a dream that features La Llorona, the famous Mexican tragic heroine.

CHAPTER 3

Tony in initiated by the "gang" led by the boisterous Horse. The rumors about Ultima surface in the community.

CHAPTER 4

Tony learns the value of medicinal herbs from Ultima. Plants such as oregano and osha are mentioned. Ultima teaches Tony about the Indian culture of La Nueva Espana.

CHAPTER 5

The Marez family travels to El Puerto to see Abuelo Prudencio, Maria Marez's father. Prudencio offers his views of the war.

CHAPTER 6

Tony attends school for the first time. He meets Red and Miss Maestas. After a humiliating experience, he discusses "*la tristesa de la vida.*"

CHAPTER 7

Tony's brothers return from Europe. Gabriel's dream of leaving Guadalupe for California is presented.

CHAPTER 8

Tony learns about sex from an incident involving Serrano's bull. He mentions the name "Rosie" for the second time.

QUIZ #1

Chapters 1-8

Select the correct answer (100 points).

1. This is the title of respect which the family accords to the old woman
    a. La Bruja   c. La Malinche
    b. La Grande

2. The sheriff is shot by
    a. Narciso   c. Gabriel
    b. Lupito

3. The rebellious kid that leads the gang Tony joins
   a. Bones   c. Florence
   b. Horse

4. The novel is set in this small New Mexico town
   a. Guadalupe   c. Sagrado Corazon
   b. Victoria

5. The Marez family prays to this saint
   a. St. Jude   c. Sagrado Corazon
   b. Victoria

6. Abuelo Prudencio lives in
   a. Las Pasturas   c. Las Crucas
   b. Los Alamos   d. El Puerto

7. Tony is in awe of this teacher's abilities
   a. Miss Martinez   c. Miss Maestas
   b. Los Alamos

8. Tony's brothers are in
   a. prison   c. college
   b. the Army

9. Tony's favorite brother is
   a. Leon   c. Eugene
   b. Andrew

10. Tony gets a lesson in sex education from
    a. a lecture in school
    b. his father
    c. watching the Serrano bull mate with a cow
    d. his brother's *Playboy* magazines

11. Tony is torn between these two forces within him
    a. thunder and lightning   c. moon and sea
    b. wind and sun

12. Samuel tells Tony the legend of the
    a. Cisco Kid   b. Weeping Woman
    b. Golden Carp

13. Tio Lucas surprised the Trementina sisters as they

    a. counted the money they stole in town
    b. conducted the Black Mass
    c. buried a fellow witch

14. Ultima decided to use Tony in the ritual because of his
    a. youth   c. blood
    b. innocence   d. all of the above

15. Ultima makes this a part of the ritual
    a. a concoction with snake venom
    b. three clay dolls
    c. a magic scarf of black satin

16. Tio Lucas regurgitates this strange object
    a. a ball of hair
    b. a live worm
    c. a doll's head with a pin stuck in it

17. This man accuses Ultima of being a witch
    a. Chavez   c. Tenorio Trementina
    b. Campos

18. Tony finds this object on the ground following "the test"
    a. a small gold cross   c. a lock of hair
    b. Ultima's owl

19. Tenorio is attacked by
    a. Tony's pit bull   c. Gabriel's hawk
    b. Ultima's owl

20. In the school play, Tony plays this role
    a. Baby Jesus   c. Mary
    b. Wise Man   d. a shepherd

BONUS (+5)   What is Tony's middle name?

Your answer:_____

QUESTIONS

CHAPTER 1

1. Where does the novel take place?
2. Where are Tony's brothers when the novel begins?
3. Why does Ultima come to live with the Marez family?
4. What is Jason's *secret*?
5. What prized possession does Ultima bring with her?
6. What term of endearment is used in addressing Ulima?

CHAPTER 2

1. Who is Chavez?
2. Who is Lupito?
3. What happens to the Sheriff?
4. Who is Narciso?
5. How does Lupito die?
6. Who is the important cultural heroine who appears in Tony's dream?

CHAPTER 3

1. What is the "riddle" of the first Priest in El Puerto?
2. What important *sin* is mentioned in this chapter?
3. What words are used by people to describe Ultima?
4. As part of his "initiation," Tony fights this stubborn boy — who is he and what does he look like?
5. This woman is described as evil — can you name her?

CHAPTER 4

1. What is *osha* and how is it used by the people in the pueblo?
2. Describe what these plants heal: *manzanilla* (p. 39), *oregano* (p. 37), *yerba del manso* (p. 37).
3. Tony's mother has a statue of this beautiful lady—can you name her?

CHAPTER 5

1. Where does Abuelo Prudencio live?
2. Which one of Tony's uncles comes to take them to see Abuelo Prudencio?
3. What are the names of Tony's brothers?
4. Which war is raging on in Europe, as told by Abuelo Prudencio?

CHAPTER 6

1. Gabriel describes this state as one that is ". . . flowing with milk and honey . . ." (p. 48) — can you name it?
2. Who leads Tony to first grade?
3. Who is Tony's teacher?
4. Describe Tony's lunch on the first day of school.
5. Who are George and Willy?
6. Who is the "speedy" boy whom Tony meets on the way to school?

CHAPTER 7

1. Tony's brothers will arrive from Europe to this city in California — can you name it?
2. Which one of Tony's brothers is more like Maria Luna Marez, the matriarch of the family?
3. Gabriel asks his sons if they saw *this* in California — can you name it?
4. Tony learns this "magic"— can you name it?

CHAPTER 8

1. According to his brothers, what is Tony's destined to be?
2. Tony learns about procreation by this experience — what is it?
3. The boys plan to do this as soon as possible — can you name their plan?
4. Tony hears the name of this woman and becomes curious about her — do you remember this name?

Chapters 9-16

NOTES

CHAPTER 9

Samuel talks to Tony about the legend of the Golden Carp. Gene and Leon leave home. Andrew remains at home.

CHAPTER 10

Tio Lucas is cursed by Tenorio's daughters. Ultima, confronts Tenorio. Ultima decides to use Tony as part of the exorcism to cure him.

CHAPTER 11

The garden of Narciso is discussed. The Golden Carp and the story of the Mermaid are heard by Tony from Cico.

CHAPTER 12

Ultima is accused of being a witch. She is forced to take a test from the same group of men who killed Lupito. During the "ritual," Ultima's owl attacks Tenorio. Tony discovers a mysterious pair of needles on the ground.

CHAPTER 13

Tenorio's daughter dies. The Marez family travels to El Puerto. An interesting name, "Orotea," appears.

CHAPTER 14

Tony is a shepherd in the school Christmas play. On the way home, he encounters a fight in the snow between Narciso and Tenorio. Tony hears Narciso's last confession.

CHAPTER 15

Tony's brothers return from their stay out west. Leon and Eugene talk about their accident and Las Vegas. Gabriel is more embittered than ever about his shattered dream.

CHAPTER 16

Tenorio attacks Tony. The second Trementina sister falls ill. This chapter has foreshadowing and symbolism.

QUIZ

Chapters 9-16

1. According to Ultima, witches are buried in coffins made from this tree

    a. pine   c. birch
    b. juniper   d. cottonwood

2. This man dies in the snow and asks for Tony's blessing
    a. Tenorio   c. Narciso
    b. Lupito

3. According to Ultima, the Indians did this with their dead
    a. buried them in caves
    b. mummified their remains
    c. burned their bodies and scattered their ashes

4. When the novel begins, Tony is this age:
    a. five years old   c. ten years old
    b. seven years old

5. The novel is narrated in
   a. first person   d. third person
   b. second person

6. Father Byrnes tries to teach the children the mean
   ing of this word
   a. faith   c. obedience
   b. eternity   d. sin

7. Ultima's soul is embodied in
   a. the rich, red earth   c. Tony
   b. the clay dolls   d. the owl

8. This man shoots the evil one-eyed outlaw
   a. Tio Juan   c. Tio Lucas
   b. Tio Pedro

9. In the final scene, Ultima instructs Tony to
   a. repent   c. burn her possessions
   b. forget her

10. Florence dies of
    a. pneumonia   c. accidental drowning
    b. a gunshot wound

11. This painted lady mystifies Tony
    a. Xaviera Hollander   c. Miss Maestas
    b. Rosie

12. Tony's father works for
    a. the city sanitation department
    b. the highway department
    c. the postal system

13. Tony's father had dreams of living in
    a. Arizona   c. California
    b. Colorado

14. During the confession game, Tony plays this role
    a. the priest   c. the leper shunned
    b. the sinner stoned to death   by others

15.   On his way home from the play, Tony sees these two
       figures in the snow
       a. Lupito and Chavez   c. Narciso and Tenorio
       b. Gabriel and Tio Lucas

16.   Tony plays this part in the school Christmas play
       a. a shepherd   c. a Wise Man
       b. Joseph   d. an angel

17.   This character refuses to believe in God
       a. The Vitamin Kid   c. Florence
       b. Cico

18.   During the confession game, this person has the
       ugliest confession
       a. Abel   c. Bones
       b. Horse

19.   This tribe of Indians have their spirits invaded by
       the evil witches
       a. Apaches   d. Utes
       b. Comanches   e. Navajos
       c. Mescaleros

20.   This type of tree is used in healing, according to Ultima
       a. alamo   c. weeping willow
       b. juniper

BONUS (+5) The author of this masterpiece of Chicano
Literature is this man who, by the way, is one of Dr. Baeza's
favorite novelists. Can you recall his name?

Your answer:_____

**(I WILL PROBABLY PUMMEL YOU PERSONALLY IF
YOU CANNOT ANSWER THE QUESTION!)**

QUESTIONS

CHAPTER 9

1. Which brother remains at home after the other two leave?
2. What does the Vitamin Kid call Tony?
3. Samuel relates what important folkloric *cuento*?
4. What color is the symbolic fish?
5. Tony is promoted to this grade in school — can you name it?

CHAPTER 10

1. Uncle Pedro brings this bad news to Maria Marez — what does he say?
2. Who laid the curse on Tio Lucas?
3. What did Tio Lucas witness in the clearing in the woods?
4. Where does Ultima confront Tenorio?
5. What does Ultima mold from the clay?
6. What part does Tony play in the ritual?
7. How long does the ritual last?
8. What does Ultima do with the black and gunny sack?
9. What smell arises in the last scene of the chapter?
10. What did the *brujas* use to place the curse on Tio Lucas?

CHAPTER 11

1. What oath does Tony make to Cico?
2. Cico shows Tony this beautiful sight — can you name it?
3. Who owns this breathtaking place?
4. What wondrous sight does Tony witness at the pond?
5. According to Cico, what happened to the shepherd in the *cuento* he relates?

CHAPTER 12

1. What *special* gift does Ultima give to Tony?
2. What news does Narciso give to the Marez family?
3. Who accuses Ultima of being a witch?
4. What *test* does Ultima have to pass to prove her innocence?
5. What happens to Tenorio during the argument?
6. After the horrifying incident subsides, what does Tony find on the ground?

CHAPTER 13

1. The Marez family is taking a trip — can you name their destination?
2. What type of coffin is used to bury Tenorio's daughter?
3. What does Tony envision in his dream?
4. What are *chicos*?
5. Who is Orotea?

CHAPTER 14

1. On the first day of school, what happens on the schoolyard that causes much excitement?
2. What part does Tony play in the school play?
3. Who was fighting at the Longhorn Saloon?
4. What role does Horse play in the Christmas play?
5. By following Narciso, Tony gets to see this mysterious woman — who is she?
6. What happens to Narciso?
7. What does Tony have to do for the fallen hero?
8. What happens to Tony in the horrible dream he has?
9. What happens to Ultima in the dream?
10. In the closing scenes of the chapter, the Golden Carp appears — do you remember what he did?

CHAPTER 15

1. What caused Narciso to become an alcoholic?
2. What news do Leon and Gene bring about their new Chevy?
3. Why does Gabriel have to go out into the wind?
4. Where do Tony's brothers go at the end of this chapter?
5. Why does Andrew leave, according to Tony?

CHAPTER 16

1. What story does Tony recall as he prepares to take his first communion?
2. Who is the person standing under the juniper tree?
3. What has happened to the second Trementina sister?
4. What does Tony witness in a horrible dream?
5. What sound does Tony hear when he goes to Ultima's door?

Chapters 17-22

NOTES

CHAPTER 17

In catechism, Tony learns about faith and eternity from Father Byrnes. The gang plays the "Confession Game." Tony is given the role of the priest. Florence talks about his life. The theme of existentialism is seen here. Father Byrnes uses an interesting analogy to define eternity.

CHAPTER 18

During one confession game, Tony hears the ugliest confessions from Horse and Bones. Florence refuses to confess his sins. The gang turns against Tony.

CHAPTER 19

Tony receives his first holy communion on Easter Sunday. Tony hears a "voice" within. The chapter ends with the line: "It is over . . ."

CHAPTER 20

Tellez seeks Ultima's help. Tenorio's second daughter dies. Ultima relates to Tony and Gabriel the Legend of the Comanches. The ritual puts their spirits back in the ground. Tony sees three figures in his dream — Lupito, Narciso and Florence.

CHAPTER 21

Forence drowns in Blue Lake. Heartbroken, Tony seeks solace at the end of the chapter.

CHAPTER 22

Tony is sent to El Puerto to recover from the shock of Florence's death. Tio Juan brings bad news. Tony comes across Tenorio on the way to Abuelo's house. Tenorio shoots the owl. Tony rushes home. Ultima asks Tony for one last favor before she dies. Tony recalls the events of that night and the special juniper tree.

QUIZ #3

Chapters 17-22

Please select the correct answer. Read carefully! (100 points).

1. Tenorio attacks Tony and the frightened youth re-
    members the evil man standing on the spot where he
    a. buried his daughter
    b. murdered Narciso
    c. killed Ultima's owl

2. This mysterious young man lost his mother when he
    was a baby
    a. Bones
    b. Florence
    c. Abel

3. To prove his point to the children, Father Byrnes
    uses this type of bird as an analogy
    a. sparrow
    b. robin
    c. parrot

4. Florence has this color of hair
    a. black
    b. blonde
    c. red

5.   Tony receives his first holy communion on this day
      a. Mother's Day
      b. Easter Sunday
      c. Father's Day

6   A man named Tellez seeks Ultima's help and de
      scribes a rainstorm of
      a. diamonds
      b. stones
      c. real cats and dogs!

7.   Ultima relates that this tribe of Indians lived on the
      llano of Agua Negra:
      a. Apaches   c. Mescalero
      b. Utes   d. Comanches

8.   This type of tree is used to lay the spirits of the dead
      Indians to rest
      a. cedar   c. juniper
      b. alamo   d. cottonwood

9.   Tellez wants to pay Ultima for her help, but instead
      of money she requests this
      a. a new shawl
      b. a lamb
      c. thirty pieces of silver

10.   In Chapter 21, Cico and Tony watch this phenome
      non with delight
      a. Rosie hanging her under things on the clothesline!
      b. Ultima's owl mating with another owl
      c. The Golden Carp swimming among other fish

11.   When the body of Florence is pulled up, this is at
      tached to his arm
      a. barbed wire
      b. a piece of rope
      c. a piece of heavy string

12.   To help Tony recuperate from the loss of his friend,
      the family decides to send him to
      a. El Paso   c. Las Pasturas
      b. El Puerto

13. In a horrible nightmare, Tony sees
     a. Lupito
     b. Florence
     c. Narciso
     d. all of the above

14. Tony can sense danger when Tio Juan tells Pedro that
     a. several cows have been found dead
     b. Tenorio is threatening to hurt Ultima
     c. Abuelo Prudencio is dying

15. By the end of the book, Tenorio has lost
     a. one daughter
     b. two daughters
     c. all three of his daughters

16. Tenorio shouts triumphantly that his bullet was molded by
     a. The Prince of Tides
     b. The Little Prince
     c. The Prince of Death

17. This man shoots the evil Tenorio with one shot
     a. Tío Pedro
     b. Tío Juan
     c. Tío Lucas

18. Ultima was taught her craft by
     a. God   c. a wise old man
     b. Satan   d. a Comanche
                          faith healer

19. In the closing scenes of the novel, Tony is seen burying this
     a. Ultima's shawl
     b. Ultima's Bible
     c. Ultima's owl

20.   Ultima is to be buried in a coffin made of
    a. pine   c. cedar
    b. cottonwood   d. juniper

BONUS (*el pilon*):   What is the name of the hideous horse
that Tenorio rides?

Your answer:_____

QUESTIONS

CHAPTER 17

1.   What news do the children hear about the war?
2.   Who gets into a fight in the bathroom?
3.   What happened to Florence's brothers?
4.   What word does Father Byrnes try to define for the
       children?
5.   What analogy does Father Byrnes use to make his
       point?

CHAPTER 18

1.   What special services does Tony attend at the
       church?
2.   What game do the children play on Good Saturday?
3.   Who confesses the worst sins?
4.   Who refuses to confess his sins?
5.   What happens to Tony when the gang turns against
       him?

CHAPTER 19

1. On what special day does Tony receive his First Holy Communion?
2. Among the gang members, who receives the longest penance?
3. Who is the "Voice" within Tony?
4. What will be done with the money in the collection box?

CHAPTER 20

1. What plans does Tony have for summer?
2. What victory does Tony achieve — and feels no sweetness about it?
3. What horrible story does Tellez relate about his bad luck?
4. What folk legend does Ultima related about the *llano* of Agua Negra?
5. What is the *pounding* heard on the roof of Tellez's house?
6. What structure do Gabriel and Tony build?
7. What does Ultima ask of Tellez for lifting the curse?
8. Who are the three figures in Tony's dream?

CHAPTER 21

1. Who needs to learn the legend of the Golden Carp — according to Tony?
2. What happens to Florence at Blue Lake?
3. What color of hair does Florence have?
4. What is wrapped around Florence's arm?
5. Where does Tony go to seek solace at the end of the chapter?

CHAPTER XXII

1. Who are the three figures in Tony's *last* dream?

2. Where does Tony go after Florence's funeral to rest and gather strength?
3. What is Gabriel's definition of *evil*?
4. What bad news does Tio Juan bring to El Puerto?
5. Who crosses Tony's path on the way to Grandfather's house?
6. Who is Diablo?
7. What is the spirit of Ultima's *soul*?
8. Who kills Tenorio?
9. What favor does Ultima ask of Tony in the closing scenes of the novel?
10. Where is Ultima really buried, according to Tony?

FINAL EXAMINATION

Name_____*Bless Me, Ultima*

Chicano Literature   by Rudy Anaya
Final Examination

WARNING: Do not attempt to take this exam if you have not read the novel entirely!

Part I: This exam is based on the Fiction Unit. You have read and discussed *Bless Me, Ultima* by Rudy Anaya. The questions are drawn from the reading and notes given during the study. Underline the correct answer (50 points).

1.   The setting of the novel is
    a. Las Pasturas
    b. Guadalupe
    c. Las Lunas

2.   Tony's father comes from this type of background
    a. people of the *pueblo*
    b. people of the *llano*
    c. migrant people

3.   Tony's mother comes from this type of background
    a. farmers
    b. businesspeople
    c. ranchers

4.   At the start of the novel, Tony is approximately
    a. five years old
    b. seven years old
    c. nine years old

5.   By reputation, Ultima is a
    a. faith healer
    b. witch
    c. palm reader

6.   Tony's family addresses Ultima as
      a. La Senora
      b. Abuelita
      c. La Grande

7.   Tony's brothers are in
      a. prison
      b. California
      c. Europe

8.   Ultima's companion is her
      a. faith
      b. power
      c. owl

9.   Tony's first exposure to death is through
      a. Florence
      b. Narciso
      c. Lupito

10.   This man forms a posse to track down the killer who
      shoots the sheriff
      a. Tenorio
      b. Lucas
      c. Chavez

11.   Tony's father has always yearned to go to
      a. Texas
      b. Arizona
      c. California

12.   Tony's first dream is important because he envisions
      his own
      a. birth
      b. death
      c. suffering

13.   Ultima's adversary in town is
      a. Rosie
      b. Tio Lucas
      c. Tenorio Trementina

14.   Tony is the youngest of how many children?
    a. six
    b. seven
    c. eight

15.   Tony's destiny is derived from his strange mixture of heritage combining the
    a. sun and moon
    b. earth and sun
    c. ocean and moon

16.   Miss Maestas is
    a. monolingual
    b. bilingual
    c. multilingual

17.   Ultima teaches Tony the secret of
    a. healing with herbs
    b. communicating with spirits
    c. exorcising evil spirits
    d. all of the above

18.   Samuel tells a folktale about the
    a. witches
    b. Golden Carp
    c. Indians

19.   Tio Lucas witnesses the Trementina sisters conducting a/an
    a. exorcism
    b. evil spell
    c. Black Mass

20.   Ultima decides to use Tony in the ritual because of his
    a. age
    b. innocence
    c. blood

21.   Tony's first contact with English is through
    a. his reading books
    b. Miss Maestas
    c. the red-haired boy with freckles

22.   Ultima makes these objects, which arouse Tony's curiosity
       a. *escapularios* (scapularies)
       b. herbal concoctions
       c. clay dolls

23.   In the school play, this person plays the Blessed Virgin Mary
       a. Bones
       b. Horse
       c. Florence

24.   Tony is closer to this older brother
       a. Leon
       b. Eugene
       c. Andrew

25.   This friend of Tony's does not believe in God
       a. Samuel
       b. Cico
       c. Florence

26.   This child is chosen to play the role of the priest in a game
       a. Bones
       b. The Vitamin Kid
       c. Tony

27.   This child has the most horrible confession of all
       a. Horse
       b. Bones
       c. Samuel

28.   The tribe of Indians whose spirits have been invaded by the horrible witches is
       a. Comanche
       b. Apache
       c. Mescalero

29. The type of tree that Ultima says will cure evil is
    a. oak
    b. mulberry
    c. juniper

30. This man accuses Ultima publicly of witchcraft
    a. Chavez
    b. Lupito
    c. Tenorio

31. Father Byrnes tries to teach the meaning of this difficult concept
    a. sin
    b. death
    c. eternity

32. Tony's first day in school brings changes, especially in his
    a. behavior
    b. food
    c. name

33. The town's "painted lady" is named
    a. Deborah
    b. Theresa
    c. Rosie

34. This force causes Tenorio's blindness
    a. gunshot
    b. lightning
    c. Ultima's owl

35. In the school play, Tony plays the role of
    a. St. Joseph
    b. a Wise Man
    c. a shepherd

36. The brother who stays at home to finish high school is
    a. Leon
    b. Eugene
    c. Andrew

37. The two figures in the snow that Tony sees on his
    way home from the play are
    a. Leon and Andrew
    b. the Trementina sisters
    c. Tenorio and Narciso

38. The evil Trementina used this to hurt Tio Lucas
    a. balls of fire
    b. nightmares
    c. his own hair

39. In Tony's family, they pray to this saint after supper
    a. Blessed Virgin Mary
    b. St. Jude
    c. Our Lady of Guadalupe

40. The owl symbolizes
    a. death
    b. life
    c. the soul

41. Tio Lucas regains his health by
    a. cursing
    b. vomiting a ball of hair
    c. renouncing the devil

42. Tenorio seeks revenge after losing
    a. his eye
    b. his daughter
    c. his power over others

43. Ultima passes (to Tony) her
    a. powers as a *curandera*
    b. knowledge of good and evil
    c. soul

44. To help Tio Lucas, Ultima prepared a potion using
    a. goats' milk
    b. mint leaves
    c. kerosene

45.   Tenorio's daughters are buried in this type of coffin
      a. cottonwood
      b. oak
      c. pine

46.   To prove her innocence, Ultima has to
      a. leave her family
      b. renounce her powers
      c. pass a test

47.   Tony buries the owl under
      a. an oak tree
      b. an elm tree
      c. a juniper tree

48.   Tellez swears that he saw this strange sight
      a. ghosts of dead Indians
      b. balls of fire on his roof
      c. a hailstorm of rocks

49.   Lupito is
      a. retarded
      b. schizophrenic
      c. both of the above

50.   The first priest who settled in the area was believed
      to be a/an
      a. Luna
      b. Marez
      c. ancestor of Ultima's family

Part II: The second part of the exam focuses on some of the "key" scenes of the novel. How is your memory by now? Concentrate! (50 points).

51.   Tony's lunch at school was
      a. sandwiches on white bread
      b. *tacos de tortilla con frijoles y chile*
      c. cafeteria food unknown to him

52.   Tony's brothers return home only to decide to
      a. re-enlist

   b. return to school
   c. leave for California
53.   Tony learns about sex when he sees
   a. his brother's pornographic magazines
   b. Rosie and her prostitutes
   c. a cow and bull copulating

54.   Tony discovers that the Vitamin Kid is related to
   a. Horse
   b. Bones
   c. Samuel

55.   In his class, Tony is the
   a. oldest
   b. slowest
   c. smartest

56.   Tony learns that some witches take the form of
   a. crows
   b. owls
   c. coyotes

57.   When Tio Lucas surprises the witches, he protects himself by
   a. running away
   b. hiding behind a tree
   c. making a cross with branches

58.   To cure Tio Lucas, Ultima will be paid
   a. twenty pesos
   b. forty pesos
   c. fifty pesos

59.   Ultima's "test" to prove her accuser wrong involves
   a. herbs
   b. candles
   c. needles

60.   Tony's serious illness comes as a result of
   a. his confrontation with Tenorio
   b. his exposure to snow and ice
   c. a curse placed on him

61. Little is done to investigate Narciso's death since he is a
    a. coward
    b. criminal
    c. drunk
62. Rumor had it that Narciso died under a/an
    a. pine tree
    b. oak tree
    c. juniper tree

63. Tony's brothers did not make it to California but settled in
    a. Albuquerque
    b. Las Vegas
    c. Santa Fe
64. The *existentialist* among Tony's friends is
    a. Samuel
    b. Cico
    c. Florence

65. Tony's "reward" for listening to his friends' confessions is
    a. popularity
    b. a rosary
    c. a beating

66. Florence has
    a. blonde hair
    b. red hair
    c. brown hair

67. In a nightmare, Tony sees these figures
    a. Narciso and Lupito
    b. Lupito and Florence
    c. Narciso, Lupito, and Florence

68. By the end of the novel, Tenorio has lost
    a. one daughter
    b. two daughters
    c. three daughters

69. This man kills the evil Tenorio
    a. Uncle Juan
    b. Uncle Pedro
    c. Gabriel Marez

70.   Tenorio knows that Ultima's strength lies in:
        a. her power to heal people
        b. her reputation in town
        c. her owl

71.   Tony's last words to Ultima are
        a. "forgive me . . ."
        b. "you cannot die . . ."
        c. "Bless me, Ultima."

72.   Ultima instructs Tony to
        a. bury her possessions
        b. burn her possessions
        c. keep her possessions

73.   Ultima is buried in a
        a. cottonwood coffin
        b. pine coffin
        c. juniper coffin

74.   The novel employs this style of narration
        a. first person
        b. third person
        c. omniscient narration

75.   The author of this novel currently resides in
        a. Albuquerque
        b. Santa Fe
        c. Las Cruces

Bonus: Can you name the award that was given to the author of for this top selling novel soon after its publication? (5 points)

Your answer:_____

Part III: This is the "self-expression" part of the exam. Write a short composition (100-150 words) on the following topic: (25 points)

Why is *Bless Me, Ultima* a novel of initiation?

Ultima Meets
the Press

Profile of a Writer, Teacher, Parent and Mentor
by Jeffrey McDonald

reprinted from *The Fort Stockton Pioneer* 4/27/95

You may not have had the pleasure of meeting author Rudolfo Anaya in person. But you can meet the man through his work, and learn about the life that has produced what the *El Paso Times* called "one of the best writers in the country."

Today, Anaya is an internationally-published writer and a world lecturer, a career educator and an inspiration to thousands of young people, some of whom have pursued successful writing careers of their own.

But before all that he was a boy growing up in a small community in rural New mexico, a boy who found his identity in his family, his friends, his experiences and his faith.

"Well, I was born and raised here in New Mexico, specifically in Santa Rosa, which is about two hours east of Albuquerque," said Anaya. "And at this point, being raised as a child around World War Two, I had probably most of the experiences that children in a small town do. And this meant participating as a family member, and going to school, and going to church, and playing childhood games with my friends."

"But I was also very fortunate to be raised along the Pecos River, in a small town with lots of space and close to nature. And very early, I paid attention a great deal to nature and the spirit of nature. And that living spirit of the river and the hills made its way into my novel, into *Bless Me, Ultima.*

In that novel, as we read of young Antonio Marez and his struggle to identify his self and his place in the world, we also read of his attempts to reconcile God's hand at work in nature with the conflicting stories of his friends and with the knowledge that there is also evil at work in the world. It is a struggle that a young Anaya experienced himself.

"It was my first novel. And in it I was reflecting upon the beliefs of the people," he explained. "And one thing that is very clear in a long tradition of Hispanic folk tales is the struggle between good and evil. And very often the belief that there are people in the world that are called witches, and certain things are ascribed to them. And I find that belief very interesting, because it has a great deal to tell us about the spiritual world."

"And beginning with *Bless Me, Ultima*, I was exploring a boy's life through a very ordinary 'coming-of-age' tale. but at the same time I was also exploring his spiritual life. So I often find it puzzling to find people who object to an exploration of that spiritual life. For me, things are not painted in one absolute version that answers all questions. Therefore, writing, for me, has been a way of answering those questions. And I think the novel, *Bless Me Ultima*, will help young people reflect upon those questions in their own exploration of their spiritual life."

It is a belief – and a faith in the intelligence and the fortitude of our young people – that Anaya has seen affirmed repeatedly over the past twenty years since the release of his first novel.

"Students can understand this, and I can document that," he said. "I receive letters from all over the country. Teachers will have their students write to me. And I'm very impressed that young people understand the novel, they understand the conflicts of its characters. And they also understand that the boy [Marez] is wrestling with the questions of good and evil, and why evil exists in the world."

"And I gather from the letters that the students write that they are engaged in these same questions. And they're not getting the answers from television or the movies, where you get these '30-minute answers'. Those answers don't satisfy them. And I am gratified that literature still has something to say to them. And I think that is what literature is all about, satisfying these questions that we ask."

While Anaya may not use the angry language that a few Fort Stockton critics used in condemning his work, he does share the concern that all parents have for their child's growth and education. And he urges all parents to be active participants in that process.

"Somebody recently asked me, 'don't you get mad when people object, when parents object to their children reading your work?' And I said to them, 'of course not. I have a twelve-year-old granddaughter, and I'm very involved in her choices, her education, her life and her reading. And I want her to be able to reflect on her own life in some of the things she reads.' So I'm very much in favor of an active role parents play in their children's life and their education."

"I think what I object to is when one or two persons find something, maybe one or two things, objectionable. And they don't read it, they don't read the entire novel," he added. "And they want to censor the book for these very small reasons that they extract from the entire novel. I think that if the novel is read in its entirety, then I think people will realize that it is a search for answers and an exploration of a spiritual life. So what I find unfair is the censorship that can occur from one or two persons that haven't read the whole novel, or grasped its meaning."

It is an issue that has touched Anaya closely, and which he addresses not only as a writer and a parent, but also as an educator and a mentor.

"I think it's important for people to know that I have been a teacher all my life. That is what I was trained for, and I have taught at kindergarten, elementary school, high school, and in the university," said Anaya, who retired two years ago from his position of Professor of Literature at the University of New Mexico. "And I really think education has to be an open forum for ideas. One way to train our young people to live and function in a multi-cultural world, and to understand the world and the different groups and communities, is to read. And I am sold on that."

"And for me, the negative is when people want to close off that discussion because they have a different point of view, or they come from a different community. I don't think we can afford that sort of closed thinking or closed mentality in the world we live in."

It is a world in which Anaya continues to be an active participant. He describes the two years since his retirement from the university as the busiest he has ever known. *The Anaya Reader*, an anthology of his short stories, essays and plays, was released earlier this year and another novel is due out in just two months. Two more novels are "in the computer and ready to go!"

He and his wife recently returned from a six-city, six-university lecture tour of Italy, where his works are now being prepared for publication in Italian. Closer to home, he and his wife are proud grandparents and active participants in their granddaughter's upbringing.

"My life is also still that of a teacher, and we're so busy writing," he said. "And at one point, I said, ' wouldn't it be nice to retire from retirement!' "

But Anaya is still a man of the llano and the valley, one who sees himself as a neighbor and a friend to all of us here in West Texas who live along the Pecos River, who have enriched his life and his art.

"I wish to send my best regards to all the good people there, along the south Pecos River, in Texas!"

Chicano author Anaya documents evolving Latino culture in his work
by Robert L. Halpern

reprinted from *The Big Bend Sentinel* 4/2/92

Rudolfo Anaya has become the male alter ego of Ultima, the central character in his most powerful novel, *Bless Me, Ultima.*

She's little Antonio's grandmother, the *curandera* for the people of northern New Mexican villages where Antonio grew up, on the mysterious, magical *llano.*

Like Antonio, Anaya was raised on the llano.

Ultima is one of the last living links to *Atzlan* — the unknown homeland for Latinos in the North and South Americas and Mexico — dispensing wisdom, warnings and guidance, serving as a continuum of a history and culture of a people.

During a roundtable discussion with the noted Chicano author at the Alpine Community Center Saturday afternoon, Anaya transformed into a sage, an elder, a wise one, himself now a continuum of a culture, challenging the small group of participants with his views of the local, regional and global villages, of politics, the state of life, education and evolving culture of American Latinos.

Roundtable participants could have been sitting in the shade made by a *lechuguilla*-stalk porch of an old adobe chanti, stuck out in Far West Texas nowhere, a scene, if you will, out of *Bless Me, Ultima,* or one of the short stories, called *cuentos,* in his book, *The Silence of the Llano.*

Life and death, represented by the seasons and the elements are an integral part of Antonio's and Anaya's life and culture, and right on cue, a storm grew outside south Alpine that cloudy, clammy Saturday afternoon, with lightning, light rain and howling winds, a foreboding of the coming of la llorana that night.

Are we Chicanos, Latinos, Hispanics, Mexicans, Mexican-Americans, Spanish-Americans, Mestizos? a roundtable participant asked.

Labels, labels, labels, Anaya sighed, and then he answered, yes, to the question.

"Why can't we be bi-cultural or even multi-cultural, I think we can," he said, noting that Latinos (et cetera) in the 90s are a co-mingling of peoples and cultures from Europe and the Americas, from white to black to every shade in between.

He debunks the lighthearted academic sociologist 'parachute theory' that the Spaniards dropped from the sky into the New World, bringing with them the Catholic religion and other cultural, social and agricultural aspects, but leaving themselves and that of the indigenous North Americans untainted by each other.

Said Anaya: It's the nature of man and woman to, uh, mingle.

Anaya came of age in the ethic hotbed of the political 1960s, during the rise of Chicano power and Hispanic awareness. He remains one of only a handful of Chicano writers.

That awareness and the struggle for the promotion of the old, the new and the evolving Latino culture must continue, he said.

"Our culture is evolving, it's mot static. Our roots are not just many streams," the University of New Mexico at Albuquerque English professor said.

But other new Latinos are rediscovering their heritage, he said, citing as an example a woman he knows in New Mexico, a registered nurse, who now is learning the ways of the curandera, that is, a multi-cultural holistic approach to her profession, her culture, her life.

Other aspects of the current culture concern him.

"We're losing the Spanish language," he observed, "a process that began in World War II. The assimilation process is very fast and devastating."

A major problem, he said, is the public education system.

"They've never presented our history or culture. That's the struggle, to learn about it and feel proud of it."

Antonio — and Anaya — are products of multi-culturalism and the struggle of old and new ways, a theme further explored in his new book, *Albuquerque.*

In *Ultima,* Antonio, and in his autobiography, Anaya, is the offspring of a restless vaquero father and mother whose roots are in a village of farmers.

Anaya's own life personifies the new and evolving Latino culture: Monolinguistic in the Spanish tongue as a child, learning English and assimilating into the Anglo culture in public school. His wife is Anglo. He writes in English. Saturday's roundtable discussion was in English.

Yet Anaya still is promoting the rediscovery of his and others' roots in his books and writings, in his lectures and in his state of mind.

Anaya's new book explores the latest evolution in the Chicano culture as the characters in the book are offspring of a Mexican father and an Anglo mother.

It's a topic that's getting positive feedback from those who have read the book.

"Hey, you're writing about me," he said a multi-cultural Latino friend recently told him.

Appendix

"Place many juniper branches on the platform. Cut many branches because we may have to burn a long time. Have Antonio cut them, he understands the power of the tree —"

— Bless Me, Ultima, p. 222

MEDICINAL HERBS FOUND IN

BLESS ME, ULTIMA

One interesting cultural assignment to give is to make a list of medicinal herbs which are presented in the novel. Below you will find a list of the herbs and their medicinal uses.

1. **Juniper (*Juniperous Ssp)*—a small shrub, 4–6 feet high, found growing in bands of limestone. In the Southwest, juniper is used to cure headaches, influenza, nausea, and spider bites. Indians used the clear smoke of burning juniper wood for feasting and ceremonial fires. To help a patient recovering from a long illness, the medicine man and his assistants made gestures of casting the disease away, similar to *la cura del susto*(cure for fright). In both rituals, the patient's body is "swept" with either a juniper or lilac branch, thus expelling the evil forces. The juniper tree is mentioned repeatedly in *Ultima* during key scenes.

Consult Eliseo Torres' book, *Green Medicine: Traditional Mexican-American Herbal Remedies* (Nieves Press, Kingsville, Texas, no date given) for further information on the juniper tree. He states that juniper berries are used to ". . . combat bad odors and, legends say, evil influences as well" (p. 40).

2. **Oregano *(wild marjoram)*** — Ultima teaches Tony the importance of this herb, which is used to relieve tension, sore throats, and bronchitis.

3. **Pine *(Pino)*** — according to the traditions

"Ultima   and   I walked in the hills of the llano, gathering the wild roots and herbs for her medicines."
    — *Bless Me, Ultima, p. 36*

"For Ultima, even the plants had a spirit..."
    — *Bless Me, Ultima, p. 37*

"Of all the plants we gathered none was endowed with so much magic as the yerba del manso."
    — *Bless Me, Ultima, p. 37*

"We were also lucky to find osha, because this plant grows better in the mountains.
    — *Bless Me, Ultima, p. 37*

found in *Ultima,* women who are rumored to be witches are buried in coffins made of pine. The juice from pine trees is used to cure cough and chest infections. Pine needles soaked in water are said to help restore energy.

4. **Rosemary *(Romero)*** — aside from correcting indigestion in babies, the tea made from this herb is believed to increase a person's memory. Indians of the Southwest used it to cure arthritis and sore muscles. Tony is given herbal teas by Ultima during times of stress and fright to calm him down.

5. **Osha *(Ligusticum Poteri)*** — the Indians of the Southwest used this herb as a good luck charm, equivalent to the four-leaf clover associated with St. Patrick's Day. It grows best in New Mexico and Southern Colorado. Alfred Savinelli, in his book, *Plants of Power* (Native Scents, Inc., Taos, New Mexico, 1993), states, "Wayfaring Native Americans have carried Osha Root as a talisman to ward off rattlesnakes and witches' spells" (p. 36).

6. **Yerba del manso** (*manso* can translate as *calm* or *quiet* in this instance; my faithful Velasquez Dictionary also defines *manso* as a "man who cares for goats and sheep") — used for all universal ills. Tony says it best when he describes the herb in this manner: "It cures coughs, or colds, cuts and bruises, rheumatism, and stomach troubles, and my father once said the old sheep herder used it to keep poisonous snakes away from their bedrolls by sprinkling them with *osha* powder" (*Ultima,* p. 37).

You may want to collect pictures of the herbs mentioned in the novel for display. If you have an herbarium in your vicinity, you may decide to arrange a field trip to enable your students to observe the plants.

I also suggest that you consult an interesting M.A. thesis that I located in the Bryan Wildenthal Memorial Li-

"*There were some plants that Ultima could not obtain in the* llano *or the river, but many people camr to seek cures from her and they brought in exchange other herbs and roots. Especially prized were those plants that were from the mountains.*"

— *Bless Me, Ultima, p. 39*

"It was peaceful under the juniper tree . . . The tree's huge, dark branches offered protection, like a confessional."

— *Bless Me, Ultima, p. 162*

brary entitled "Medicinal Plants of the Trans-Pecos Area," written by Evalina A. Soza in 1970 (Sul Ross State University, Alpine, Texas). It has an impressive list of herbs and their medicinal value. Students can even prepare herbal teas during the unit to add creativity and practicality to the study. They can also create their own herbariums by bringing a sample herb to class for extra points.

Possible Topics For *Bless Me, Ultima* Essays and Projects

1. Tony Marez as a Christ symbol in the novel.

2. Existentialist undertones in Anaya's novel.

3. Anaya's portrayal of women in *Ultima*.

4. Maria Marez as a Madonna symbol.

5. The Outsiders of Guadalupe: Rosie, Lupito, Florence.

6. Folk remedies found in *Ultima*.

7. Cultural symbols: la Llorona and the Legend of the Golden Carp.

8. Guadalupe in *Ultima* and Thalia in Larry Mc-Murtry's *The Last Picture Show*: a comparative study of life in a small town.

9. Miss Maestas: a bilingual/bicultural teacher's approach to teaching Spanish-dominant children.

10. Narciso's garden: Eden in the desert.

11. World War II as seen through the eyes of the Marez boys.

12. Lupito: Anaya's version of Forrest Gump in Guadalupe.

13. Anaya's use of supernatural effects in *Ultima*

14. The concept of "La Familia" in *Ultima*

15. Anaya's interesting use of names and nicknames (*nombres y apodos*).

16. Ultima: the prototype of "La Abuelita" (the Midwife-Granny).

17. Anaya's use of stream-of-consciousness in *Ultima*.

18. Historical fiction as seen in *Bless Me, Ultima*.

19. Analogy and symbolism in *Ultima*.

20. *Bless Me, Ultima* as a novel of initiation.

21. Rosie: the quintessential "Painted Lady" as social outcast.

22. Tenorio Trementina and Shakespeare's Macbeth: woes, foes, and witches.

23. Horse, Bones, and "the gang": Guadalupe's "home-boys."

24. Anaya's use of cultural rituals in *Ultima*.

Glossary of Terms

(Arranged in the order that they appear in the novel)

vaqueros	cowboys
llaneros	plainsmen
mamá	mother
curandera	shaman, faith healer
chingada	damned, cursed
cabrón	male goat, ram
ristras	string of peppers
cabritos	kid goats
tío	uncle
mis hijos (also spelled *mijos*)	my sons
perdón	pardon, excuse me
llano	plains
papá	father
la muerte	death
abuelo (also spelled *guelo, guelito*)	grandfather
vieja	old woman
bruja	witch
atole	gruel made of corn or wheat flour, milk, and cinamm-
caballeros	gentlemen, horsemen
jodido	cursed, damned
mierda	defecation, waste
borracho	drunk
puto, puta	prostitute
pendejo	dummy, Forrest Gumpish
muchacho	lad
sangre	blood
jefa (literally means "lady boss")	Mother
purga	laxative
pesadilla	nightmare
brujería	witchcraft

Glossary of Expressions

(Arranged in the order in which they appear in the novel)

Está sola . . . . (She) is alone
Ya no queda gente en el pueblo . . . . . No one is left in town
¡Qué lástima! . . . . What a pity!
Es verdad . . . . It's true
Ave María Purísima . . . . Hail Mary most holy
Está bien . . . . Very well
La Grande . . . . Grand Dame
¿Donde está (Jason)? . . . . Where is Jason?
Buenos días le de Dios . . . . Good day to you
La Virgen de Guadalupe . . . . Our Lady of Guadalupe
Un momento . . . . Just a minute
¡Ándale, hombre, ándale! . . . . Move it, man, move it!
Mataron a mi hermano . . . . . Someone killed my brother
Ya vengo . . . . I'm coming
¿Qué pasa? . . . . What's happening?
Pero, ¿qué dices, hombre? . . . . . What are you saying, man?
¡Lo mató, lo mató! . . . . (He) killed him!
Jesús, María, y José . . . . Jesus, Mary, and Joseph
Por Dios, hombres . . . . By God, men
mi Toñito . . . . my little Tony
Ven acá . . . . Come here
Vamos . . . . Let's go
En el nombre del Padre, del Hijo,
    y del Espíritu Santo . . . . In the name of the Father,
                                            Son, and Holy Ghost
la tristeza de la vida . . . . the sadness of life
Gracias a Dios . . . . Thanks be to God
Cuidado . . . . careful
Saludos a papá y a todos! . . . . . . Greetings to Dad and all!
Gracias por mi vida . . . . Thank you for my life
Es sin pecado . . . . (she) is without sin
A la veca . . . . I'll be damned!
¡Ay, Dios! . . . . Oh, God!
¿Quién es? . . . . Who is it?
¡La mujer que no ha pecado

es bruja, le juro a Dios! . . . . . . The woman who has not
sinned is a witch, I swear to God!
¡Chinga a tu madre! . . . . Damn your mother!
Mira . . . . Look
¡Madre mia! . . . . Mother of mine!
Te voy a matar, cabrón! . . . . I'll kill you, bastard!
¡Ay, que Diablo! . . . . That Devil!
cabrones putas . . . . damned whores
¡Voy a tirar tripas! . . . . I'm gonna blow chunks!
¡Gracias por Dios que venites! . . . . . Thank you for coming!
(formal Spanish would be *veniste*)
yerba de la víbora . . . . snake weed
Le doy la bendicíon en el nombre . . . I bless you in the name
del Padre, Hijo, y del . . . . of the Father, Son, and
Espíritu Santo . . . . Holy Ghost
¡Hijo de la bruja! . . . . Son of the witch!

Selected Bibliography

Alves Pereira, Teresinha. "Review of *Bless Me, Ultima*, by Rudolfo A. Anaya. *Hispamerica:Revista de Literatura*, No. 4-5 (1973): 137-39.

Anaya, Rudolfo A. "Antonio's First Day of School." *Pace* (1983): 146-49.

————. *Bless Me, Ultima*. Berkeley, CA: Quinto Sol, 1972. 249 pp.

————. *The Legend of La Llorona*. Berkeley, CA: Tonatiuh-Quinto Sol International, Inc., 1984. 95 pp.

Bauder, Thomas A. "The Triumph of White Magic in Rudolfo Anaya's *Bless Me, Ultima*." *Mester*. 1985 Spring; 14(1): 41-54.

Calderon, Hector. "Rudolfo A. Anaya's *Bless Me, Ultima*. A Chicano Romance of the Southwest." *Critica*. 1.3 (1986): 21-47. Rpt. *Rudolfo A. Anaya: Focus on Criticism*. Ed. Cesar A. Gonzales-T. La Jolla, CA: Lalo Press, 1990.

Cantu, Roberto. "Apocalypse as an Ideological Construct: The Storyteller's Art in *Bless Me, Ultima*." *Rudolfo A. Anaya: Focus on Criticism*. Ed. Cesar A. Gonzales-T. La Jolla, CA: Lalo Press, 1990.

Cinader, Maud. "Rudolfo Anaya's *Bless Me, Ultima* as a Gesture of Trust." Unpublished paper, June 1988.

Dutchover, Mary L. "Rudolfo A. Anaya's Multicultural Aspects in *Bless Me, Ultima* and *Heart of Aztlan*." Unpublished paper submitted as class project. Sul Ross State University, 1993.

Gish, Robert F. "Curanderismo and Witchery in the Fiction of Rudolfo A. Anaya: The Novel as Magic." *New Mexico Humanities Review*, 2, No. 2 (Summer 1979): 5-12.

Hall, Rosanna. "Author Teaches Chicano Novel, Writes of Man's Violent Nature." *The El Paso Times* 22 September 1979: sec. C.

Lamadrid, Enrique R. "Myth as the Cognitive Process of Popular Culture in Rudolfo Anaya's *Bless Me, Ultima*: The Dialect of Knowledge." *Hispania* 1985 September; 68(3): 496-501.

Mondin, Sandra. "The Depiction of the Chicana in *Bless Me, Ultima* and *The Milagro Beanfield War*: A Study in Contrasts." *Mexico and the United States: Intercultural Relations in the Humanities*. Ed. Juanita Luna Lawhn, et. al. San Antonio: San Antonio College, 1984.

Pickett, Rebecca. "Bless Me, Ultima: A Chicano Novel for Young Adults." Southwest Texas State University, n.d.

Ray, J. Karen. "Cultural and Mythical Archetypes in Rudolfo Anaya's *Bless Me, Ultima*," *New Mexico Humanities Review*, l, No. 3 (September 1978), 23-8.

Rodrigues, Raymond J. "*Bless Me, Ultima* by Rudolfo A. Anaya." In "A

Novel, Poem, Story, Essay, to teach." Comp. Susan Kock. *English Journal*, 65, No. 1 (January 1976): 63-64.

Rogers, Jane. "The Function of the *la llorona* Motif in Rudolfo Anaya's *Bless Me, Ultima*." *Latin American Literary Review* 10(1977): 64-69.

Sarkissan, Adele, ed. "Rudolfo A. Anaya: An Autobiography." *Contemporary Authors: Autobiography Series*. 4(4) 1986, 15-28. The Gale Research Company.

Unpingco-Garrett, Regina. "Images of Women in *Bless Me, Ultima*." *Vision*. (Spring 1976): 41-42.

Urioste, Donaldo. "The Child Protagonist in Chicano Fiction." Dissertation. University of New Mexico. 1985.

Waggoner, Amy. "Tony's Dreams — An Important Dimension in *Bless Me, Ultima*." *Southwestern American Literature*, IV (1974): 74-79.

Zimmerman, Enid. "An Annotated Bibliography of Chicano Literature: Novels, Short Fiction, Poetry, and Drama. 1970-1980." The Bilingual Review/Revista Bilingue 9.3 (1982): 231-32.

Quiz Answers

Quiz #1	*Quiz #2*	*Quiz #3*
1. B	1. A	1. B
2. B	2. C	2. B
3. B	3. C	3. A
4. A	4. B	4. B
5. B	5. A	5. B
6. D	6. B	6. B
7. C	7. D	7. D
8. B	8. A	8. C
9. B	9. C	9. B
10. C	10. C	10. C
11. C	11. B	11. A
12. B	12. B	12. C
13. B	13. C	13. C
14. D	14. A	14. B
15. B	15. C	15. B
16. A	16. A	16. C
17. C	17. C	17. A
18. B	18. B	18. C
19. B	19. C	19. C
20. C	20. B	20. A

Final Examination Answers

1. B	26. C	51. B
2. A	27. A	52. C
3. A	28. A	53. C
4. B	29. C	54. C
5. A	30. C	55. C
6. C	31. C	56. C
7. C	32. C	57. C
8. C	33. C	58. B
9. C	34. C	59. C
10. C	35. A	60. B
11. C	36. C	61. C
12. A	37. C	62. C
13. C	38. C	63. C
14. B	39. C	64. C
15. C	40. C	65. C
16. B	41. B	66. A
17. D	42. B	67. C
18. B	43. B	68. B
19. C	44. C	69. B
20. B	45. C	70. C
21. C	46. C	71. C
22. C	47. C	72. A
23. B	48. C	73. A
24. C	49. C	74. A
25. C	50. A	75. A